Crypto Empire Crumbled

The BitBoy Saga And The Volatile World Of Digital Wealth

Richard H. Graham

Table Of Contents

Introduction

The development of cryptocurrency influencers in the digital era, primarily via platforms like YouTube, marks a fundamental shift in how financial information and investment advice are shared and consumed.

These influencers have utilized the vast reach and accessibility of digital media to position themselves as authoritative figures within the Bitcoin community, affecting both market patterns and individual investment choices.

YouTube, with its large user base and algorithm-driven video distribution, has emerged as a significant medium for bitcoin influencers.

It provides a unique blend of visual and audio material delivery, making complicated subjects like blockchain technology and cryptocurrency investing more accessible to a larger audience. Influencers leverage YouTube's capabilities, such as live streaming, video series, and community interaction tools, to establish and retain a loyal following.

Rise Of Personalities Like BitBoy

Personalities like Ben Armstrong, nicknamed BitBoy, have seized on the platform's potential to construct captivating tales around their crypto adventures. They give insights on market trends, investment ideas, and the newest news inside the crypto industry, frequently merging personal experiences with professional advice.

This blend of personal branding and professional coaching has been incredibly beneficial in developing a persona that audiences trust and connect to.

Influence Within The Crypto Community

The effect of these people goes beyond essential content production. They actively affect market views and investing habits. Through their recommendations, evaluations, and speculative forecasts, influencers may drive attention toward specific cryptocurrencies, ICOs (Initial Coin Offerings), and blockchain projects.

Their views typically have weight, resulting in substantial market moves depending on their endorsements or critiques.

However, this influence comes with its problems and obligations. The fragmented and extremely volatile character of the cryptocurrency market renders it subject to disinformation and speculative enthusiasm. Influencers, then, wield a tremendous commitment to guarantee truth, openness, and ethical consideration in their work.

The growth of influencers like BitBoy has generated talks about the need for governmental control and ethical rules to safeguard customers from possible fraud and disinformation. The digital era, pioneered by platforms like YouTube, has fostered the growth of cryptocurrency influencers who play a vital role in educating, informing, and influencing the crypto community.

While they give valuable insights and help democratize financial information, their rising impact emphasizes the need for higher accountability and ethical norms in the quickly changing crypto sector. As the industry continues to expand, the role of these influencers will likely shift, reflecting changes in legal frameworks, market dynamics, and audience expectations.

Chapter One: The Birth Of BitBoy

Early Life And The Road To Crypto Stardom

Ben Armstrong's path from an ordinary Joe to a cryptocurrency phenomenon is a narrative of redemption, reinvention, and the tireless pursuit of success despite all obstacles. Born in a humble, middle-class household, Armstrong's early life was far distant from the glamor and glamor associated with the world of Bitcoin today.

From an early age, Armstrong exhibited an entrepreneurial drive, engaging in several projects with varied degrees of success and failure. However, it was his meeting with the dark side of addiction that proved to be a turning point in his life.

Battling methamphetamine addiction, Armstrong touched rock bottom before he found the courage to pull himself out of the abyss. This journey not only tested his fortitude but also influenced his future ethos.

Armstrong's entry into the realm of cryptocurrencies was not a deliberate choice but a chance finding during his pursuit of financial independence and a solid livelihood. Initially hesitant, he eventually grew absorbed with the subtleties of blockchain technology and the transformative possibilities of digital currency.

It was a period when the crypto market was still in its infancy, riddled with volatility and uncertainty. Still, Armstrong saw an opportunity for atonement and a chance to rebuild his life on his terms.

The Formation Of The BitBoy Brand

The birth of the BitBoy brand was a planned decision motivated by Armstrong's ambition to carve out a position in the expanding crypto market.

Recognizing the potential of social media and video production, he aimed to demystify cryptocurrencies for the public, utilizing YouTube as his platform of choice.

The pseudonym "BitBoy" was iconic, a fun homage to the digital nature of cryptocurrencies, and a character that was both accessible and memorable.

In the early days, the BitBoy channel was a one-person show, with Armstrong scripting, shooting, and editing his films. His material was a combination of market analyses, investing suggestions, and courses on crypto trading and mining.

What set Armstrong apart was his ability to break down complicated topics into digestible, compelling information, making the arcane realm of crypto accessible to newcomers and experts alike.

As the BitBoy channel increased, so did its effect. Armstrong's direct, no-nonsense style, combined with his deep insights into market patterns, gained him a dedicated following.

The BitBoy brand became associated with trustworthy crypto guidance, and Armstrong, the face behind it, emerged as a thought leader in the sector.

The Lamborghini Dream: Symbol Of Success

For Armstrong, success in the crypto market was not only about money rewards but also about showing himself and the world that he could rise beyond his history. The purchasing of a Lamborghini Huracán Performante became the actual representation of this triumph, a concrete sign of his journey from poverty to riches.

The Lamborghini was more than simply a luxury automobile; it was a monument to the force of tenacity, hard work, and the revolutionary potential of Bitcoin.

The day Armstrong took receipt of the Lamborghini was a moment of victory, not only for him but also for his admirers, who saw in his accomplishment a light of optimism.

The automobile, with its sleek design and screaming engine, became a recurring element in BitBoy's material, a continuous reminder of what was possible in the crypto realm. However, the Lamborghini was also a double-edged sword.

While it functioned as a symbol of success, it also garnered criticism and jealousy, with opponents accusing Armstrong of flaunting his money and deceiving his followers with get-rich-quick scams.

Yet, for Armstrong, the Lamborghini remained a personal milestone, a prize for years of work, and a monument to the life-changing potential of cryptocurrencies.

The genesis of BitBoy is a narrative of change, a journey from the depths of despair to the heights of digital celebrity. Ben Armstrong's early life, defined by difficulties and obstacles, created the basis for a career that would later make him a household figure in the crypto world.

Establishing the BitBoy brand was a smart move, harnessing the power of social media to educate and inspire. And the Lamborghini dream, although a sign of prosperity, also acted as a reminder of the instability and criticism inherent in the bitcoin realm.

Armstrong's tale is not only a narrative of personal triumph; it is a testimony to the democratizing potential of the internet and digital currency.

Through the BitBoy platform, Armstrong has provided a doorway into the intricate world of Bitcoin, making it accessible to anyone. In doing so, he has not only carved out a spot for himself in the digital pantheon. Still, he has encouraged numerous others to investigate the possibilities of blockchain technology and digital currencies.

Chapter Two:The Golden Era Of Crypto Influence

The climb of cryptocurrencies from a niche interest to a popular sensation has been nothing short of spectacular, with the digital revolution finding its champions in the shape of influencers. Among them, YouTube channels devoted to cryptocurrencies have emerged as crucial platforms, giving insights, assistance, and a feeling of community to both newcomers and veterans of the crypto industry.

In this golden period of crypto influence, personalities like Ben Armstrong, better known as BitBoy, have become prominent, exploiting their expertise and charm to transform the landscape of crypto investing.

The Rise Of Cryptocurrency YouTube Channels

The rise of cryptocurrency YouTube channels can be traced back to the early days of Bitcoin when digital money was a matter of fascination for many. As the promise of blockchain technology and cryptocurrencies started to unravel, a new genre of video makers developed, devoting their channels to demystifying this complicated world for the public.

These channels differed in their approach, with some focused on the technical elements of blockchain technology, while others gave market assessments, investing suggestions, and news updates.

The attractiveness of YouTube as a platform for crypto influencers resides in its accessibility and the immediacy of its content. Viewers may now obtain real-time information on market movements, learn about developing currencies, and gain insights into trading tactics, all in an appealing video format.

This democratization of knowledge played a significant part in the broad acceptance of cryptocurrencies, making what was formerly an obscure issue accessible to a worldwide audience.

BitBoy's Strategies And Influence On Crypto Investments

Among the forefront of crypto influencers, BitBoy built a unique niche for himself via a mix of slick marketing, strategic content development, and an innate awareness of his audience's requirements.

Armstrong's approach to constructing the BitBoy brand was comprehensive, focused not only on content quality but also on creating a character that viewers could trust and connect to. One of BitBoy's primary goals was to provide instructional information and market research, appealing to both novices and seasoned traders.

He boiled complicated topics into consumable portions, frequently utilizing analogies and simple language to illustrate sophisticated elements of Bitcoin trading and investing. This made his channel a go-to resource for anyone navigating the unpredictable crypto markets.

Moreover, BitBoys timing was flawless. His rise to prominence coincided with heightened interest in cryptocurrencies, spurred by Bitcoin's bull runs and the ICO mania.

By continuously delivering important insights and timely guidance, Armstrong established himself as a thought leader in the sector.

Partnerships, Promotions, And The Price Of Fame

As the BitBoy channel increased, so did prospects for collaborations and marketing with burgeoning crypto projects and enterprises.

These relationships were not only profitable but also assisted Armstrong in growing his influence inside the crypto community. However, they also created new obstacles, notably in preserving openness and ethical norms.

The crypto influencer industry is plagued with potential conflicts of interest, with influencers being accused of supporting projects in which they have a financial interest without appropriate transparency.

Armstrong negotiated this problematic situation by being careful in his collaborations and seeking to retain honesty with his audience.

However, the very nature of influencer marketing in the crypto world meant that charges of prejudice and evil advertising were never far away. The price of popularity in the crypto influencer realm is very costly.

As BitBoy's impact rose, so did scrutiny and criticism. The unpredictable nature of bitcoin investments means that losses are inevitable, and influencers like Armstrong typically suffer the brunt of their followers' displeasure during market downturns.

Furthermore, the continuous growth of the crypto ecosystem needs influencers to adapt and refresh their expertise continually, a formidable challenge that Armstrong did with grace.

The golden age of crypto influence has been marked by the birth of a new breed of financial advisors: the crypto influencers. Platforms like YouTube have played a significant part in this transition, offering a forum for influencers like BitBoy to share their expertise, insights, and forecasts with a worldwide audience.

Armstrong's journey through this terrain provides excellent lessons on the power of strategic content production, the value of ethical alliances, and the obstacles to attaining credibility in a quickly changing industry.

As the world of Bitcoin continues to expand, the role of influencers will likely alter with it. However, the influence of personalities like BitBoy on the uptake and understanding of cryptocurrencies will remain a crucial chapter in the history of digital money.

Their capacity to demystify complex technology, guide investment choices, and develop communities around similar interests has been essential in the mainstreaming of cryptocurrencies, marking a transformational time in the digital age.

Chapter Three: The Shadows Behind The Spotlight

In the realm of Bitcoin, where innovation and speculation collide, figures like BitBoy have lit the road for millions.

Yet, this bright path is not without its shadows, created by the delicate dance of ethics, scandals, and regulatory scrutiny.

The crypto realm, with its decentralized ethos and quick expansion, has frequently found itself at war with conventional financial norms, creating a complicated scenario for influencers traversing its terrains.

The Blurry Lines Of Financial And Personal Ethics In Crypto

Cryptocurrency, by design, defies traditional financial institutions, functioning in a sphere where anonymity and decentralization are embraced. This new frontier has drawn pioneers and prospectors alike, but it has also highlighted problems about the ethical bounds of financial advice and influence.

For influencers like BitBoy, these ethical issues are twofold: they must negotiate both their integrity and the economic well-being of their audience. Personal ethics in the crypto world frequently focus on openness and honesty.

Influencers carry considerable influence, capable of altering market emotions with a single tweet or video. The responsibility that accompanies this power cannot be stressed.

Ethical difficulties occur when personal benefits are placed against audience trust. The desire to advocate high-risk ventures or enterprises in which one has a concealed financial interest is a persistent concern.

Financial ethics further blur when influencers become de facto counselors to their audience. The decentralized nature of crypto means that regulatory structures and safeguards that exist in conventional finance are frequently missing or unenforced.

This adds extra weight on influencers to behave in their audience's best interest, avoiding promoting speculative investments without explicit caution about possible hazards.

The Controversies: Unstable Coins And Undisclosed Promotions

The crypto sector is no new to problems, many of which have entangled individuals at the vanguard of the industry. Unstable coins, or cryptocurrencies with little to no underlying value, have been a particular flashpoint.

The attraction of rapid riches has led to the rise of such coins, frequently supported by aggressive marketing efforts.

Influencers, caught in the crossfire of excitement and optimism, have occasionally found themselves pushing these unstable commodities, resulting in severe financial losses for their followers.

Undisclosed promotions intensify this problem, blurring the boundary between accurate advice and compensated endorsement. The quick ascension of crypto has seen a spike in companies aiming to leverage influencer reach.

However, the omission to disclose financial links with these ventures misleads followers and weakens the trust crucial to an influencer's reputation.

Instances of influencers being detected in such secret advertisements have led to public reaction, wasting audience confidence and ruining reputations long established on honesty and openness.

Regulatory Shadows And The SEC's Gaze

The rising significance of cryptocurrencies inside financial markets has not been ignored by regulatory organizations, most notably the U.S. Securities and Exchange Commission (SEC). The SEC's duty to safeguard investors and preserve fair, orderly, and efficient markets sets it squarely in conflict with the uncontrolled wilderness of crypto.

This issue has increasingly placed influencers under the SEC's eyes since their marketing and endorsements frequently interact with securities regulations.

The SEC's worry principally focuses on the potential for fraud and manipulation inside the crypto market, with influencers playing a significant role in molding investor behavior. The lack of clarity on what defines security in the crypto realm adds complexity to these regulatory difficulties.

Influencers working in this gray area find themselves negotiating a delicate road, balancing the promotion of innovation with the possibility of regulatory reaction.

The shadows created by regulatory monitoring have led to a delicate dance between influencers and the SEC.

High-profile incidents where influencers have faced legal action for their activities in marketing unregistered securities have acted as a sharp reminder of the regulatory constraints that remain, even in decentralized marketplaces.

These cases have triggered reevaluating procedures within the influencer network, focusing more on compliance and transparency.

The shadows behind the limelight in the crypto influencer realm testify to the complicated interaction of ethics, scandals, and legislation.

As pioneers in a new financial frontier, influencers like BitBoy negotiate an environment where the enthusiasm for invention frequently collides with the realities of accountability and regulatory compliance.

The path through these shadows is not only about avoiding traps but also about creating the future of cryptocurrencies. By addressing the ethical challenges, engaging controversies head-on, and respecting legal frameworks, influencers may reveal a way that is both creative and secure.

The crypto industry sits at a crossroads, with the acts of influencers today determining the norms and standards of tomorrow.

As the sector evolves, the lessons acquired from navigating these shadows will be vital in developing a crypto community that values openness, honesty, and responsibility.

The spotlight that once exposed a world of unimaginable possibilities now also underlines the need for a balanced approach to crypto impact, one that appreciates the power of this new financial age while realizing the responsibility it brings.

Chapter Four: Downfall Of An Empire

In cryptocurrencies, fortunes may fluctuate as swiftly as the markets themselves. The case of Ben Armstrong, better known as BitBoy, is a harsh reminder of how steep the fall can be from the height of digital glory.

Armstrong's evolution from a lauded influencer to a person immersed in controversy and legal disputes offers a warning story about the volatility of cryptocurrencies and the very nature of popularity and influence within this developing sector.

The Fall From Grace: Loss Of Wealth, Reputation, And Relationships

BitBoy's fall from glory was not a solitary event but a sequence of blunders and disasters that destroyed the basis of his empire. The early signals of problems came with the erratic swings of the crypto market, which saw Armstrong's wealth change rapidly, echoing the uncertain character of the commodities he had championed.

However, the loss of riches was only the beginning. More detrimental was the deterioration of his reputation, triggered by several incidents that called into doubt his ethics and integrity as an influencer.

As Armstrong's techniques and proposals were investigated, so did his intentions. Allegations of concealed advancements and conflicts of interest emerged, portraying a man more concerned with personal wealth than his followers' welfare.

This story was further fanned by the unstable currencies and enterprises he was accused of supporting, generating enormous financial losses for individuals who had put their confidence in his guidance.

The human cost of Armstrong's professional difficulties was considerable. Relationships developed over the years, both inside the crypto world and in his personal life, started disintegrating. Friends and associates withdrew, while the mounting public outcry added pressure to his personal life.

The guy who had previously been hailed for his insights and contributions to the crypto world suddenly found himself ostracized, a pariah inside the same community he had helped to construct.

The Ousting From HIT Network: A Tale Of Betrayal

The most severe blow to Armstrong's empire, however, came from inside. The ouster from HIT Network, the firm he had co-founded and grown into a cornerstone of his reputation, was a dramatic turn of events that many regarded as the climax of his fall from grace.

The facts of the ouster are buried in charges of treason and internal power battles, portraying a picture of a partnership undone by distrust and avarice.

The issue at the core of the expulsion was complicated, encompassing arguments about the firm's direction, financial management, and Armstrong's behavior. Allegations of misused finances and unscrupulous business practices occurred, leading to a protracted fight for control of HIT Network.

The final dismissal of Armstrong from the organization was not only a professional defeat; it was a public spectacle that further degraded his image and underlined the precariousness of his position within the crypto industry.

Legal Battles And Allegations: The Tumultuous End Of An Era

The dismissal from HIT Network was only the beginning of Armstrong's legal difficulties. In the aftermath, a succession of lawsuits and claims arose, trapping him in a web of legal disputes that threatened to absorb what remained of his fortune and authority.

This litigation, ranging from claims of fraud and slander to disagreements over intellectual property, formed an image of a man beleaguered on all fronts. The charges against Armstrong were severe, touching on both his professional methods and personal conduct.

Accusations of sexual harassment and workplace misbehavior added a dark element to the drama, distorting the narrative of an essential fall from financial grace. As the court fights stretched on, the toll on Armstrong's mental and emotional well-being became more apparent.

Public declarations and social media postings presented a guy striking out against perceived injustices but simultaneously wrestling with the tremendous implications of his predicament on his personal life and identity.

The stormy conclusion of Armstrong's career was not merely the tale of a guy undone by the fickle world of Bitcoin.

It mirrors the more significant issues confronting the crypto community, exposing the ethical dilemmas, regulatory uncertainty, and personal hazards inherent in this new frontier of money.

Armstrong's breakdown serves as a warning reminder of the fragility of celebrity and power in a profession distinguished by its unpredictability.

The breakdown of BitBoy's empire is a narrative distinguished by tremendous highs and tragic lows. It is a tale that underlines the precarious junction of human ambition, financial speculation, and digital celebrity. As Armstrong navigates the repercussions of his fall from grace, his narrative remains a striking reminder of the dangers and benefits that come with the terrain of Bitcoin's influence.

The legacy of BitBoy's growth and collapse is multifaceted, acting as both a warning and a lesson for the crypto world. It underlines the significance of openness, ethics, and integrity in a field that remains largely unregulated and sometimes misunderstood.

For Armstrong, the voyage is far from done. The route to redemption, if it exists, will entail a confrontation with the faults of the past and a determination to restore trust in a future where the shadows of controversy no longer loom large.

Chapter Five: The Personal Cost Of Digital Fame

The rise and fall of Ben Armstrong, known to the digital world as BitBoy, weaves a story much beyond the volatility of cryptocurrency markets—it's a tragic tale of the emotional cost of digital stardom.

Armstrong's transition from a recognized crypto influencer to a figure involved in controversy and court fights serves as a sobering reminder of the fragility of digital popularity and its effect on one's personal life and well-being.

The Midlife And Spiritual Crisis Of Ben Armstrong

For Armstrong, the ramifications of his public image and the accompanying issues were not merely financial and professional but emotionally personal. As his kingdom started to disintegrate, so did the internal scaffolding of his identity and purpose.

The obsessive pursuit of success in the digital sphere drove him into what can best be characterized as a midlife and spiritual crisis—a time defined by reflection, remorse, and a yearning for purpose outside the limitations of cryptocurrencies and digital celebrity.

This crisis was marked by significant doubts about the worth of his work and the legacy he intended to leave behind. The character of BitBoy, once a source of pride and identity, became a mask that Armstrong found more challenging to wear.

The discrepancy between his online image and his internal battle intensified feelings of isolation and detachment, not only from the crypto community but from his sense of self.

The spiritual nature of this catastrophe cannot be underestimated. Armstrong found himself wrestling with profound problems about morality, honesty, and redemption—themes that transcended the monetary achievement he had earned.

This phase of spiritual reckoning pushed him to examine the effect of his activities on others and the ethical implications of his influence in the crypto world.

The Impact On Family: Divorce And Personal Turmoil

Perhaps the most devastating consequence of Armstrong's fall from grace was on his family. The public issues and court fights took a considerable toll on his relationships, ending in a divorce that highlighted the final human cost of his digital stardom. The dissolution of his marriage was not simply a private sorrow but a public spectacle, adding to the weight of an already tricky moment in Armstrong's life.

The effect on his family stretched beyond the collapse of his marriage. The relentless media attention and public outrage damaged the lives of his children, exposing them to the harsh reality of their father's public image.

Armstrong's issues with identity, purpose, and ethics were not simply his own. Still, they were shared, in part, by his family, who had to negotiate the aftermath of his digital celebrity alongside him.

This era of emotional upheaval was punctuated by periods of reflection and remorse as Armstrong pondered the toll his work had taken on the people closest to him.

The revelation that his quest for achievement and notoriety had come at the price of his family's well-being was a painful admission, requiring him to face the repercussions of his actions in a profoundly personal manner.

Rebuilding From The Ashes: Attempts At Redemption

In the wake of his career and personal failure, Armstrong started on a path of atonement, aiming to rebuild his life and legacy from the ashes of his previous empire. This route was not only about returning financial stability or professional reputation but about restoring his integrity and establishing a sense of purpose that transcended the digital stardom that had previously defined him.

Armstrong's efforts atonement entailed a determined attempt to reconnect with his family, restore shattered connections, and construct a new foundation focused on honesty, humility, and ethical behavior.

He wanted to reinvent his identity beyond BitBoy, concentrating on personal development, spiritual healing, and a dedication to making atonement for previous misdeeds.

This road of redemption also found Armstrong participating with the crypto community in new ways, valuing education and advocacy above speculation and excitement.

He became increasingly outspoken about the ethical concerns inside the crypto industry, utilizing his profile to advocate responsible investing and to advise against the temptations that had earlier entrapped him.

The human cost of internet fame for Ben Armstrong is a story of loss, contemplation, and the desire for atonement. It illustrates the enormous influence that pursuing success in the digital arena can have on one's personal life, relationships, and sense of self.

Armstrong's experience serves as a cautionary tale about the fragility of online popularity and the significance of basing one's identity on principles and connections that transcend the unpredictable realm of Bitcoin.

As Armstrong continues to rebuild from the ashes of his past life, his path provides vital lessons about the power of redemption, the significance of ethical behavior, and the eternal worth of personal integrity.

In the end, Armstrong's legacy may likely be characterized not by the heights of his digital fame but by the depth of his devotion to establishing a new path—one distinguished by humility, compassion, and a revitalized sense of purpose.

Chapter Six: The Crypto Community's Reckoning

In the vast, ever-evolving environment of cryptocurrencies, the narrative of Ben Armstrong, also known as BitBoy, is more than a personal saga—it's a mirror reflecting the more significant issues and ethical quandaries confronting the crypto community. His rise and fall capture the unpredictable nature of digital currencies, the impact on essential people, and the aftermath of scandals that have left lasting scars on the sector. This chapter goes into the ripple consequences of Armstrong's path, the more considerable repercussions of crypto controversies, and the lessons that may build a more responsible future for influencers within this area.

The Ripple Effect: How BitBoy's Story Reflects Larger Industry Issues

BitBoy's tale is a microcosm of the crypto world's intricacies, showcasing how individual acts may echo throughout the network.

Armstrong's journey to popularity and subsequent scandals illustrate the incredible power of influencers in changing market dynamics, driving investment patterns, and, at times, contributing to speculative bubbles.

His experience highlights crucial issues about the duty assumed by those who steer public opinion and investment in an environment as risky and uncontrolled as cryptocurrencies.

The blurring borders between personal benefit and public guidance illustrated by Armstrong's trip reflects a more significant industry issue: the need for openness and ethical standards.

The crypto sector, praised for its decentralization and anonymity, typically works in murky regions of legality, leaving it ripe for conflicts of interest.

Armstrong's participation in numerous projects without full disclosure demonstrates the hazards of influencer marketing in the crypto industry, where the line between impartial advice and compensated advocacy may frequently be muddy.

The Aftermath Of Crypto Scandals: FTX And Beyond

The difficulties surrounding BitBoy did not occur in isolation but amid a time defined by multiple high-profile crypto scandals, with the collapse of FTX being the most famous.

These instances have not only resulted in enormous financial losses for investors but have also generated a crisis of trust in the crypto market. They underline the weaknesses inherent in the Bitcoin ecosystem, including challenges of governance, transparency, and the hazards of centralized control masked behind a decentralized narrative.

The aftermath of these incidents has significantly influenced the crypto community, sparking demands for more robust regulation and monitoring.

The instance of FTX, in particular, emphasized the perils of celebrity endorsements and influencer marketing in affecting investment choices without fully comprehending the underlying issues.

These episodes serve as sharp reminders of the necessity for due diligence, regulatory compliance, and the crucial role of trust in maintaining the crypto ecosystem.

Lessons Learned And The Path Forward
For Crypto Influencers

The stormy experiences of Armstrong and the larger crypto community provide valuable lessons for influencers and players in the digital currency world.

The first is the vital necessity of transparency. Influencers must properly declare their affiliations with the initiatives they advocate, ensuring their audience is aware of any biases.

This dedication to openness is not simply ethical but vital to preserving confidence and credibility.

Secondly, the need for education and critical thinking in the crypto realm has never been more essential. Influencers have a duty not just to advocate initiatives but also to educate their audience on the intricacies and hazards involved with Bitcoin investing.

By cultivating a better-educated community, influencers may help lessen the effect of conjecture and avoid the repeat of previous errors. Finally, the route ahead for crypto influencers entails a transition towards a more sustainable and ethical paradigm of influence.

This involves lobbying for and complying with industry standards and regulatory norms, encouraging initiatives with true promise and value, and prioritizing the long-term health of the crypto ecosystem above short-term advantages. The tale of BitBoy and the larger narrative of crypto scandals have acted as a wake-up call for the cryptocurrency ecosystem, stressing the essential need for ethical standards, transparency, and regulatory clarity.

As the business continues to evolve, the role of influencers will be examined more than ever, putting a premium on individuals who can handle the intricate interplay of innovation, investment, and integrity.

The future of cryptocurrencies hinges not only on technical improvements but also on developing a culture of accountability and trust. Influencers, as the connection between the crypto industry and the larger public, are crucial in defining this future.

By learning from the past and adopting a path of ethical influence, they may help lead the crypto community toward a more stable, trustworthy, and inclusive future.

Chapter Seven: The Future Of Cryptocurrency Influence

The cryptocurrency ecosystem is ever-evolving, impacted by industry trends, technology breakthroughs, and the changing sands of regulatory frameworks.

In this dynamic environment, influencers hold significant power, driving investment choices and creating perceptions. However, the aftermath of the crypto boom and the issues that have plagued the sector call for a reevaluation of the role and duties of these digital leaders.

As we look into the future, many significant patterns emerge, suggesting the route ahead for cryptocurrency impact.

Navigating The Post-Boom Landscape Of Crypto

The phenomenal expansion of cryptocurrencies has been both a gift and a burden, leading to unprecedented interest and investment and instability and speculative bubbles.

As the dust settles from this frantic activity, the crypto community finds itself at a crossroads, seeking stability and sustainability in the post-boom age.

This new terrain needs a detailed grasp of the market's intricacies and the elements that drive value beyond simple speculation. Influencers, therefore, must adapt to this changing environment, concentrating on promoting a more excellent grasp of blockchain technology's potential and the real-world uses of cryptocurrencies. This change entails shifting away from hype-driven marketing to a more calculated strategy that prioritizes long-term growth and usefulness.

The post-boom scenario also gives a chance to reestablish trust. After experiencing the consequences of many scandals and market collapses, the crypto community desires stability and dependability.

Influencers may play a vital part in this recovery process by advocating projects with sound foundations, open operations, and clear value propositions.

Ethical Considerations And The Need
For Transparency

The future of Bitcoin's impact is closely related to ethical questions and the demand for openness. The previous activities of specific influencers, plagued by secret promotions and conflicts of interest, have underlined the necessity for a moral compass in leading the community.

Transparency is not only a statutory necessity but a core aspect of trust. Influencers must be transparent about their relationships and the nature of their recommendations, enabling their audience to make educated judgments.

This clarity extends to the initiatives, as influencers argue for transparency in operations, governance, and financial transactions.

Moreover, the ethical landscape of crypto influence comprises the obligation to preserve the community's interests.

This role entails careful investigation before approving initiatives, refuting erroneous claims, and presenting balanced perspectives that understand potential and hazards. By following these rules, influencers may help develop a more mature and discriminating crypto community.

The Evolving Role Of Influencers In Shaping The Crypto World

As we look to the future, the role of influencers in the crypto industry is primed for significant development. No longer simply pundits or promoters, influencers are becoming educators, activists, and thought leaders, helping the community through the complexity of blockchain technology and its ramifications for society.

This shift mirrors a more significant trend toward value-driven influence. In the crypto realm, this involves focusing on initiatives that give advantages, such as promoting financial inclusion, strengthening privacy, or supporting decentralization.

Influencers are well positioned to spotlight these initiatives, attracting attention to novel uses of blockchain technology that may solve real-world concerns. In addition, the future will undoubtedly see influencers taking a more active part in lobbying and regulatory talks.

As the connection between the crypto community and the larger public, influencers can help create the narrative surrounding cryptocurrencies, pushing for fair and pragmatic rules that protect investors while stimulating innovation.

The expanding function of influencers also entails cooperation and community development. By working together and using their platforms, influencers may build a more unified and robust crypto economy.

This collaborative approach may help magnify critical ideas, challenge disinformation, and encourage a culture of learning and exchange within the community.

The future of cryptocurrency influence is filled with possibilities, distinguished by the possibility to push the sector towards a more ethical, transparent, and value-driven future.

As the crypto landscape navigates the difficulties and opportunities of the post-boom period, influencers stand at the vanguard, possessing the capacity to shape perceptions, influence choices, and create significant change. The route ahead demands a commitment to openness, ethical behavior, and community welfare.

By adopting these ideals, influencers may help push the Bitcoin community toward a better future defined by trust, innovation, and inclusion. In doing so, they will not only redefine their responsibilities within the crypto ecosystem but also contribute to the development and stability of the sector as a whole.

Conclusion

The narrative of Ben Armstrong, known to the world as BitBoy, illustrates the breakneck journey of cryptocurrencies from the edges of the internet to the forefront of global banking.

His rise and fall are a microcosm of the broader crypto tale, filled with quick ascents, catastrophic collapses, and the ever-present promise of regeneration.

As we reflect on the legacy of BitBoy, it becomes evident that his narrative provides insights and cautions for the future of cryptocurrencies, digital riches, and the influencers who navigate this unpredictable world.

The Legacy Of BitBoy: Insights And Warnings From A Cautionary Tale

BitBoy's narrative is a cautionary tale that emphasizes the intricacies and hazards of digital celebrity in the era of Bitcoin. His transition from an ardent promoter of digital currencies to a person engaged in scandal demonstrates the problematic balance between power and accountability.

The lessons obtained from his trip shed light on the necessity of ethical standards, transparency, and the need for a powerful moral compass in the quest for digital riches. One of the glaring cautions of BitBoy's legacy is the possible repercussions from unrestrained influence.

As bitcoin continues to catch the imagination of investors and fans alike, the role of influencers comes under more scrutiny. Armstrong's experiences remind us that with great power comes great responsibility—a proverb that is especially true in the speculative and sometimes opaque realm of cryptocurrencies.

Moreover, BitBoy's narrative serves as a heartbreaking reminder of the human consequences connected with digital stardom.

The toll on relationships, mental health, and personal integrity may be tremendous, highlighting the necessity for a balanced approach to life in the public spotlight.

These observations and cautions are crucial as the crypto community goes ahead, delivering lessons that may influence future actions and plans.

The Ongoing Evolution Of Cryptocurrency And Digital Wealth

Cryptocurrencies are in a perpetual state of upheaval, driven by technology developments, legal shifts, and the ever-changing dynamics of global finance.

The emergence of digital wealth is distinguished by both possibilities and problems, as the potential for innovation competes with the requirement for stability and confidence.

As blockchain technology improves, we are seeing the rise of increasingly complex uses of cryptocurrencies, from decentralized finance (DeFi) to non-fungible tokens (NFTs) and beyond.

These advances promise to reshape the idea of digital wealth, widening its reach beyond just cash to cover a wide variety of digital assets. However, the continued development of Bitcoin is also riddled with obstacles. Issues of scalability, interoperability, and environmental sustainability remain vital barriers.

Moreover, the issue of regulatory ambiguity remains large as governments and financial institutions battle with how to incorporate digital currencies into the current financial system without strangling innovation.

Looking Ahead: The Future Of Crypto Influence And Regulation

The future of cryptocurrencies is intrinsically related to the twin powers of influence and regulation. As the industry grows, the role of influencers like BitBoy is anticipated to expand, moving towards a more instructional and advising capacity.

The focus will likely change from speculative investing to fostering awareness and appropriate involvement in the crypto community. This change will need a tighter connection with regulatory frameworks as openness and accountability become key.

The crypto community, including influencers, developers, and investors, must participate in constructive communication with regulators to build an atmosphere that combines innovation with consumer protection.

Looking forward, we may foresee a more regulated cryptocurrency market, defined by more precise standards for participation and investment.

This legislative clarification might open the way for further use of digital currencies as conventional financial institutions, and the broader public develop trust in the stability and validity of the crypto market.

The future also offers the potential for further decentralization, as blockchain technology allows more egalitarian and accessible financial institutions.

In this picture of the future, the effect of digital wealth goes beyond investment returns, contributing to larger social objectives such as financial inclusion and economic empowerment.

The legacy of BitBoy, with its combination of insights and cautions, provides a blueprint for navigating the complex world of Bitcoin. As the community thinks about the lessons learned from his experience, the route ahead is defined by cautious hope.

The continual growth of digital wealth and the regulatory environment provide both difficulties and opportunities for crafting a more stable, inclusive, and inventive future for Bitcoin.

In this scenario, the influence exerted by personalities like BitBoy may be a force for good, directing the crypto community towards responsible development and significant contribution to the global economy.

As we look forward, the lessons of the past act as a lighthouse, lighting the path ahead in the ever-evolving adventure of cryptocurrencies.

www.ingramcontent.com/pod-product-compliance
Lightning Source LLC
Chambersburg PA
CBHW071101290526
45795CB00004B/1604